THE ROYAL COURT THEATRE PRESENTS

What If If Only

by Caryl Churchill

What If If Only was first performed at the Royal Court Jerwood Theatre Downstairs, Sloane Square, on Wednesday 29 September 2021.

What If If Only
by Caryl Churchill

CAST (in alphabetical order)

Linda Bassett
John Heffernan
Jasmine Nyenya or **Samir Simon-Keegan**

Director **James Macdonald**
Designer **Miriam Buether**
Lighting Designer **Prema Mehta**
Sound Designer **Christopher Shutt**
Assistant Director **Grace Duggan**
Stage Manager **Heather Cryan**
Deputy Stage Manager **Fran O'Donnell**
Costume Supervisor **Jackie Orton**
Chaperone **Victoria Renoldi-King**
Set built by **Ridiculous Solutions**
Video Content **Isaac Madge**

From the Royal Court, on this production:

Casting Director **Amy Ball**
Company Manager **Joni Carter, Alex Constantin**
Production Manager **Marius Rønning**
Stage Supervisor **Steve Evans**
Lighting Supervisor **Cat Roberts**
Lead Producer **Catherine Thornborrow**
Sound Supervisor **David McSeveney**

The Royal Court and Stage Management wish to thank the following for their help with this production:
Jackie De Panizza (UK SOBS), Caroline Meer.

What If If Only
by Caryl Churchill

Caryl Churchill (Writer)

For the Royal Court: **Glass. Kill. Bluebeard. Imp., Escaped Alone, Pigs & Dogs, Love & Information, Seven Jewish Children, Drunk Enough To Say I Love You?, A Number, Far Away, This is a Chair, Blue Heart, Mad Forest, Ice Cream, Serious Money, Fen, Top Girls, Cloud 9, Traps, Light Shining in Buckinghamshire, Owners.**

Other theatre includes: **Here We Go, The Skriker (National).**

Music theatre includes: **Lives of the Great Poisoners, Hotel (both with Orlando Gough).**

Caryl has also written for radio & television.

Linda Bassett (Cast)

For the Royal Court: **Escaped Alone, Love & Information, In Basildon, Wastwater, The Stone, Lucky Dog, Far Away, The Recruiting Officer, Our Country's Good, Serious Money, East Is East (& Tamasha/Birmingham Rep/Theatre Royal, Stratford East); Aunt Dan & Lemon (& Public, NYC), Abel's Sister, Fen (& Almeida/Joint Stock/Public, NYC/Tour).**

Other theatre includes: **People, Schism in England, A Place with the Pigs (National); A Winter's Tale, Pericles, Henry IV Part I & II, The Theban Plays, Artists & Admirers (RSC); Roots, Phaedra (Donmar); Richard III, The Taming of the Shrew (Globe); Visitors (& Bush/UK tour), Road to Mecca (Arcola); Love Me Tonight, Out in the Open (& Birmingham Rep), The Awakening (Hampstead); The Bald Prima Donna, Medea (& Leicester Haymarket/Almeida), The Seagull (Liverpool Playhouse); The Cherry Orchard (Leicester Haymarket); The Clearing (Bush); Hortensia & the Museum of Dreams (Finborough); Five Kinds of Silence (Lyric, Hammersmith); The Triumph of Love (Almeida/Tour); Interplay (Leeds Playhouse/Belgrade TIE, Coventry).**

Television includes: **Call the Midwife, The Life & Adventures of Nick Nickleby, Spies of Warsaw, Grandma's House, Larkrise to Candleford, Sense & Sensibility, The Brief, This Little Life, Our Mutual Friend, Kavanagh QC, Far from the Madding Crowd, Silent Film, Christmas, A Touch of Frost, A Small Dance, No Bananas, Newshounds, A Village Affair, Bramwell, Loved Up, Skallagrig.**

Film Includes: **Effie, West is West, Cass, The Reader, Kinky Boots, Separate Lies, Calendar Girls, The Hours, The Martins, Don Quixote, East is East, Beautiful People, Oscar & Lucinda, Paris By Night, Waiting for the Moon.**

Miriam Buether (Designer)

For the Royal Court: **Glass. Kill. Bluebeard. Imp., The Children (& MTC/Broadway), Escaped Alone (& BAM, NYC), Love & Information (& NYTW), Get Santa!, Sucker Punch, Cock, In the Republic of Happiness.**

Other theatre includes: **King Lear, To Kill a Mockingbird, Three Tall Women, A Doll's House Part 2 (Broadway); Hymn, and breathe..., Shipwreck, Machinal, Albion, Boy, When the Rain Stops Falling, Judgement Day (Almeida); The Jungle (& West End/St Ann's, NYC/Curran, San Francisco), Red Demon, The Bee (& Japan), The Trial, Public Enemy, Wild Swans, The Government Inspector, In the Red & Brown Water, The Good Soul of Szechuan, Generations (Young Vic); Sunny Afternoon, Chariots of Fire (& Hampstead), Bend It Like Beckham (West End); The Father (Theatre Royal, Bath); The Effect, Earthquakes in London (National); Six Characters in Search of an Author (Chichester Festival/West End); Guantanamo: Honor Bound to Defend Freedom (Kiln/West End/Off-Broadway/San Francisco); The Cherry Orchard (Amsterdam).**

Dance includes: **Frame of View (Cedar Lake, NYC).**

Opera includes: **La Fanciulla Del West (& Santa Fe Opera), Turandot, Wozzeck (ENO); Anna Nicole (& NYC), Suor Angelica (ROH); The Death of Klinghoffer (Edinburgh Festival Fringe/Scottish Opera).**

Awards include: **The Linbury Prize for Stage Design; Evening Standard Best Design Awards (Earthquakes in London, Sucker Punch, The Jungle).**

Grace Duggan (Assistant Director)

Theatre includes: **after birth (North Wall); Lysistrata (Arcola); Wood (VAULT Festival).**

Grace directs the Junior Youth Theatre at Theatre Royal Stratford East and works with community groups around the UK.

John Heffernan (Cast)

For the Royal Court: **Love & Information.**

Other theatre includes: **A Slight Ache, Carrie's War, The Hothouse (West End); Saint George & the Dragon, Edward II, She Stoops to Conquer, Emperor & Galilean, After the Dance, The Habit of Art, The Revenger's Tragedy, Major Barbara (National); Macbeth (Young Vic); Oppenheimer (& West End), King Lear, The Seagull, King John, Romeo & Juliet, Much Ado About Nothing (RSC); The Physicists (Donmar); The Last of the Duchess (Hampstead); Richard II (Tobacco Factory); Love, Love, Love (Paines Plough); Lloyd George Knew My Father (Theatre Royal, Bath).**

Television includes: **Becoming Elizabeth, The Pursuit of Love, Dracula, Game of Thrones, Brexit: The Uncivil War, Collateral, The Crown, The Loch, Dickensian, Luther, Jonathan Strange & Mr Norrell, Ripper Street, The Suspicions of Mr Whicher, Outlander, Foyle's War, Love & Marriage, Murder on the Home Front, Henry IV Part I & II,The Shadow Line, King Lear.**

Film includes: **The Duke, Misbehaviour, Official Secrets, The Banishing, Radioactive, Crooked House, Eye in the Sky, Having You.**

Radio includes: **Doctor Faustus, Middlemarch, The National, An Ideal Husband, The Moors of England, Elsinore, A Streetcar Named Desire, The Forsyte Saga, Going Solo, Blood, Sex & Money, Home Front, Heart of Darkness, Beware of Pity, Just Dance, Shakespeare's Restless World, My Shakespeare, The Archers.**

James Macdonald (Director)

For the Royal Court: **Glass. Kill. Bluebeard. Imp., One For Sorrow, The Children (& MTC/Broadway), Escaped Alone (& BAM, NYC), The Wolf From The Door, Circle Mirror Transformation, Love & Information (& NYTW), Cock (& Duke, NYC), Drunk Enough to Say I Love You? (& Public, NYC), Dying City (& Lincoln Center, NYC), Fewer Emergencies, Lucky Dog, Blood, Blasted, 4.48 Psychosis (& St Ann's, NYC/US & European tours), Hard Fruit, Real Classy Affair, Cleansed, Bailegangaire, Harry & Me, Simpatico, Peaches, Thyestes, Hammett's Apprentice, The Terrible Voice of Satan, Putting Two & Two Together.**

Other theatre includes: **The Welkin, John, Dido Queen of Carthage, The Hour We Knew Nothing of Each Other, Exiles (National); The Night of the Iguana, Who's Afraid of Virginia Woolf?, The Father, Glengarry Glen Ross, The Changing Room (West End); True West (Roundabout/Broadway); The Way of the World, Roots (Donmar); Wild, And No More Shall We Part, #aiww – The Arrest of Ai Weiwei (Hampstead); The Father (Theatre Royal, Bath/Kiln); Bakkhai, A Delicate Balance, Judgment Day, The Triumph of Love (Almeida); The Chinese Room (Williamstown Festival); Cloud Nine (Atlantic, NYC); A Number (NYTW); King Lear, The Book of Grace (Public, NYC); Top Girls (MTC/Broadway); John Gabriel Borkman**
(Abbey, Dublin/BAM, NYC); The Tempest, Roberto Zucco (RSC); Troilus und Cressida, Die Kopien (Schaubuehne, Berlin); 4.48 Psychose (Burgtheater, Vienna); Love's Labour's Lost, Richard II (Royal Exchange, Manchester); The Rivals (Nottingham Playhouse); The Crackwalker (Gate); The Seagull (Crucible, Sheffield); Miss Julie (Oldham Coliseum); Juno & the Paycock, Ice Cream/Hot Fudge, Romeo & Juliet, Fool for Love, Savage/Love, Master Harold & the Boys (Contact, Manchester); Prem (BAC/Soho Poly).

Opera includes: **A Ring A Lamp A Thing (ROH); Eugene Onegin, Rigoletto (Welsh National Opera); Die Zauberflöte (Garsington); Wolf Club Village, Night Banquet (Almeida Opera); Oedipus Rex, Survivor from Warsaw (Royal Exchange, Manchester/Hallé); Lives of the Great Poisoners (Second Stride).**

Film includes: **A Number.**

James was an Associate and Deputy Director at the Royal Court for 14 years and was also a NESTA fellow from 2003 to 2006.

Prema Mehta (Lighting Designer)

For the Royal Court: **A History of Water in the Middle East, Superhoe.**

Other theatre includes: **The Dumb Waiter (Old Vic); Hymn (Almeida); The Comeback, A Day in the Death of Joe Egg (West End); The Winter's Tale (RSC); Swive (Elizabeth), Bartholomew Fair, Richard II (Globe); Studio Créole (Manchester International Festival); Things of Dry Hours (Young Vic); Of Kith & Kin (& Bush), Chicken Soup (Crucible, Sheffield); The Hired Man (Queen's, Hornchurch/Octagon, Bolton/Hull Truck); Fame (UK Tour/Peacock); East is East (& Northern Stage), Holes, Hercules (Nottingham Playhouse); The Importance of Being Earnest (Octagon, Bolton); Talking Heads (Leeds Playhouse); A Midsummer Night's Dream (Curve, Leicester); Mighty Atoms (Hull Truck); A Passage to India (Royal & Derngate, Northampton/UK Tour); A Christmas Carol, The Wizard of Oz (Storyhouse); The York Suffragettes, Murder, Margaret & Me (Theatre Royal, York); Love Lies & Taxidermy, Growth, I Got Superpowers for My Birthday (Paines Plough); The Effect (English Theatre of Frankfurt); Coming Up, Jefferson's Garden, Fourteen (Watford Palace); The Electric Hills (Liverpool Everyman); The Great Extension (Theatre Royal, Stratford East); The Snow Queen (Derby); The Canterville Ghost, Huddle (Unicorn); Wipers (UK Tour).**

Dance includes: **Bells (Mayor of London 2012); Spill (Düsseldorf); Sufi Zen (Royal Festival Hall); Dhamaka (O2 Arena); Maaya (Westminster Hall).**

Live events include: **A-List Party Area (Madame Tussauds, London).**

Prema is Founder of Stage Sight. She is a Trustee of the Unicorn Theatre and an Artistic Associate at the Young Vic.

Jasmine Nyenya (Cast)

Theatre includes: **Carousel (Regents Park Open Air).**

Christopher Shutt
(Sound Designer)

For the Royal Court: **Glass. Kill. Bluebeard, Imp., ear for eye, a profoundly affectionate passionate devotion to someone (-noun), Escaped Alone (& Off-Broadway), The Sewing Group, hang, Love & Information (& Off-Broadway), Kin, Aunt Dan & Lemon, Serious Money, Road.**

Other theatre includes: **Paradise, Hansard, Top Girls, Peter Gynt, Antony & Cleopatra, Julie, John, Twelfth Night, Here We Go, Man & Superman, The James Plays (I & II), From Morning to Midnight, Timon of Athens, The White Guard, Burnt by the Sun, Every Good Boy Deserves Favour, The Hour We Knew Nothing of Each Other, War Horse (& West End, Broadway, International), Happy Days, Thérèse Raquin, The Seagull, Coram Boy (& Broadway), Machinal (National); Four Quartets (Bath); Aristocrats, Saint Joan, Faith Healer, St Nicholas (& Chicago), Privacy, The Same Deep Water As Me, Philadelphia Here I Come!, Piaf (Donmar); The Merchant of Venice (Globe); The Entertainer, The Winter's Tale (West End); The Father (Theatre Royal, Bath/Kiln/West End); King Hedley II (Theatre Royal, Stratford East); Hamlet (Barbican); Bull (Young Vic); The Playboy of the Western World, All About My Mother (Old Vic); Twilight Zone (& West End), Ruined, Judgment Day (Almeida); Desire Under the Elms, Blasted (Lyric, Hammersmith); A Human Being Died That Night (& Off-Broadway), Wild (Hampstead); Shoes (Sadler's Wells); The Caretaker (Crucible, Sheffield/Kiln); Julius Caesar (Barbican); Timon of Athens, Oppenheimer (& West End), Macbeth, The Two Gentlemen of Verona, Wendy & Peter Pan, Candide, Twelfth Night, The Comedy of Errors, The Tempest, King Lear, Romeo & Juliet, Noughts & Crosses, King John, Much Ado About Nothing (RSC); Macbeth (Manchester International Festival/NYC); Drum Belly (Abbey, Dublin); Crave/4:48 Psychosis (Crucible Sheffield); Far Away, A Midsummer Night's Dream (Bristol Old Vic); Good (Royal Exchange, Manchester); Man of Aran (Druid, Galway); Country Girls, The House of Special Purpose (Chichester Festival); Little Otik, The Bacchae (National Theatre of Scotland); A Disappearing Number, The Elephant Vanishes, Mnemonic (& Broadway), The Noise of Time, The Street of Crocodiles (Complicité); Macbeth, All My Sons, The Resistible Rise of Arturo Ui, A Moon for the Misbegotten, Humble Boy, Not About Nightingales (Broadway).**

Awards include: **Tony Award for Best Sound Design of a Play (War Horse); New York Drama Desk Awards for Outstanding Sound Design (War Horse, Mnemonic, Not About Nightingales).**

Samir Simon-Keegan (Cast)

Television includes: **Paw Patrol.**

What If If Only is Samir's professional stage debut.

THE ROYAL COURT THEATRE

The Royal Court Theatre is the writers' theatre. It is a leading force in world theatre for cultivating and supporting writers – undiscovered, emerging and established.

Through the writers, the Royal Court is at the forefront of creating restless, alert, provocative theatre about now. We open our doors to the unheard voices and free thinkers that, through their writing, change our way of seeing.

Over 120,000 people visit the Royal Court in Sloane Square, London, each year and many thousands more see our work elsewhere through transfers to the West End and New York, UK and international tours, digital platforms, our residencies across London, and our site-specific work. Through all our work we strive to inspire audiences and influence future writers with radical thinking and provocative discussion.

The Royal Court's extensive development activity encompasses a diverse range of writers and artists and includes an ongoing programme of writers' attachments, readings, workshops and playwriting groups. Twenty years of the International Department's pioneering work around the world means the Royal Court has relationships with writers on every continent.

Since 1956 we have commissioned and produced hundreds of writers, from John Osborne to Jasmine Lee-Jones. Royal Court plays from every decade are now performed on stage and taught in classrooms and universities across the globe.

We're now working to the future and are committed to becoming carbon net zero and ensuring we are a just, equitable, transparent and ethical cultural space - from our anti-oppression work, to our relationship with freelancers, to credible climate pledges.

It is because of this commitment to the writer and our future that we believe there is no more important theatre in the world than the Royal Court.

**Find out more at
royalcourttheatre.com**

ROYAL

COMING UP AT THE ROYAL COURT

10 Nov–18 Dec
RARE EARTH METTLE
By Al Smith

9 Dec–22 Jan
A FIGHT AGAINST...
(UNA LUCHA CONTRA...)
By Pablo Manzi
Translated by William Gregory

21 Jan–5 Mar
THE GLOW
By Alistair McDowall

1–12 Feb
PURPLE SNOWFLAKES
AND TITTY WANKS

Written and Performed
by Sarah Hanly

Royal Court Theatre and Abbey Theatre

6 May–1 Jun
TWO PALESTINIANS
GO DOGGING
By Sami Ibrahim
Royal Court Theatre and Theatre Uncut

9–18 Jun
THE SONG PROJECT

Conceived by Chloe Lamford
and Wende in collaboration
with Isobel Waller-Bridge and
Imogen Knight, and E.V. Crowe,
Sabrina Mahfouz, Somalia
Nonyé Seaton, Stef Smith and
Debris Stevenson.

Royal Court Theatre and Stichting WENDE

RARE EARTH METTLE and THE GLOW have been generously supported with lead gifts from Charles Holloway. Further support for RARE EARTH METTLE has been received from the Cockayne Grant for the Arts, a donor advised fund of The London Community Foundation. This play is a recipient of an Edgerton Foundation New Play Award.

The development of A FIGHT AGAINST... (UNA LUCHA CONTRA...) was supported by the British Council. Teatro a Mil Foundation is a project partner.

ARTS COUNCIL ENGLAND Supported using public funding by

JERWOOD ARTS

The London Community Foundation

COCKAYNE

COURT

ROYAL

ASSISTED PERFORMANCES

Captioned Performances

Captioned performances are accessible for people who are D/deaf, deafened & hard of hearing, as well as being suitable for people for whom English is not a first language.

Is God Is: Wed 6 Oct, Wed 13 Oct, Wed 20 Oct, 7.30pm
What If If Only: Wed 13 Oct, Wed 20 Oct, 6pm
Rare Earth Mettle: Wed 1 Dec, Wed 8 Dec, Wed 15 Dec, 7.30pm
A Fight Against...(Una Lucha Contra...): Fri 7 Jan, Fri 14 Jan (English), Fri 21 Jan (Spanish)
The Glow: Wed 9 Feb, Wed 16 Feb, Wed 23 Feb, 7.30pm
Purple Snowflakes and Titty Wanks: Fri 11 Feb, 7.45pm
two Palestinians go dogging: Fri 27 May, 7.45pm
The Song Project: Fri 17 Jun, 8pm

BSL-Interpreted Performance

BSL-interpreted performances, delivered by an interpreter, give a sign interpretation of the text spoken and/or sung by artists in the onstage production

The Glow: Wed 2 Mar, 7.30pm

Audio-described Performances

Audio-described performances are accessible for people who are blind or partially sighted. They are preceded by a touch tour which allows patrons access to elements of theatre design including set and costume.

Is God Is: Sat 23 Oct, 3pm
What If If Only: Sat 23 Oct, 6pm
Rare Earth Mettle: Sat 11 Dec, 2.30pm
The Glow: Sat 5 Mar, 2.30pm

COURT

ROYAL

ASSISTED PERFORMANCES

Performances in a Relaxed Environment

Relaxed Environment performances are suitable for those who may benefit from a more relaxed environment.

During these performances:
– There is a relaxed attitude to noise in the auditorium; you are welcome to respond to the show in whatever way feels natural
– You can enter and exit the auditorium when needed
– We will help you find the best seats for your experience
– House lights may remain raised slightly
– Loud noises may be reduced

Is God Is: Sat 16 Oct, 3pm
What If If Only: Sat 16 Oct, 6pm
Rare Earth Mettle: Sat 4 Dec, 2.30pm
A Fight Against...(Una Lucha Contra...): Sat 15 Jan, 3pm
The Glow: Sat 26 Feb, 2.30pm
two Palestinians go dogging: Sat 28 May, 3pm

If you would like to talk to us about your access requirements, please contact our Box Office at (0)20 7565 5000 or boxoffice@royalcourttheatre.com
The Royal Court Visual Story is available on our website. We also produce Story and Sensory synopses which are available on request.

COURT

ROYAL COURT SUPPORTERS

The Royal Court relies on its supporters in addition to our core grant from Arts Council England and our ticket sales. 2020 was an unusual year in so many ways and we are particularly grateful to the individuals, trusts and companies who stood by us and continued to support our work during these difficult times. It is with this vital support that the Royal Court remains the writers' theatre and that we can continue to seek out, develop and nurture new voices, both on and off our stages.

Thank you to all who support the Royal Court in this way. We really can't do it without you.

PUBLIC FUNDING

Supported using public funding by
ARTS COUNCIL ENGLAND

CHARITABLE PARTNERS

JERWOOD ARTS

BackstageTrust

ORANGE TREE TRUST

CORPORATE SPONSORS

Aqua Financial Ltd
Cadogan
Colbert
Edwardian Hotels, London
Kirkland & Ellis International LLP
Kudos
SISTER

CORPORATE MEMBERS

Platinum
Auriens
Bloomberg Philanthropies

Gold
Weil, Gotshal & Manges (London) LLP

Silver
Left Bank Pictures
Patrizia
Sloane Stanley

TRUSTS & FOUNDATIONS

The Derrill Allatt Foundation
The Backstage Trust
Martin Bowley Charitable Trust
The City Bridge Trust
The Cleopatra Trust
Cockayne – Grants for the Arts
The Noël Coward Foundation
Cowley Charitable Foundation
The D'Oyly Carte Charitable Trust
Edgerton Foundation
The Golden Bottle Trust
Jerwood Arts
Kirsh Foundation
The London Community Foundation
Claire McIntyre's Bursary
Lady Antonia Fraser for the Pinter Commission
Rose Foundation
The Charles Skey Charitable Trust
John Thaw Foundation
The Victoria Wood Foundation

To find out more about supporting the Royal Court please get in touch with the Development Team at support@royalcourttheatre.com, call 020 7565 5049 or visit royalcourttheatre.com/support-us

The English Stage Company at the Royal Court is a registered charity (No. 231242)

ROYAL

BAR & KITCHEN

The Royal Court's Bar & Kitchen aims to create a welcoming and inspiring environment with a style and ethos that reflects the work we put on stage. Alongside our vibrant basement bar, you can visit our pop-up outdoor bar Court in the Square.

Offering expertly crafted cocktails alongside an extensive selection of craft gins and beers, wine and soft drinks, the Royal Court bars provide a sanctuary in the middle of Sloane Square. By day a perfect spot for meetings or quiet reflection and by night atmospheric meeting spaces for cast, crew, audiences and the general public.

All profits go directly to supporting the work of the Royal Court theatre, cultivating and supporting writers – undiscovered, emerging and established.

For more information, visit
royalcourttheatre.com/bar

HIRES & EVENTS

The Royal Court is available to hire for celebrations, rehearsals, meetings, filming, ceremonies and much more. Our two theatre spaces can be hired for conferences and showcases, and the building is a unique venue for bespoke events and receptions.

For more information, visit
royalcourttheatre.com/events

Sloane Square London, SW1W 8AS ⊖ Sloane Square ⇌ Victoria Station
🐦 royalcourt f theroyalcourttheatre ⊙ royalcourttheatre

COURT

SUPPORT THE COURT AND BE A PART OF OUR FUTURE.

Every penny raised goes directly towards producing bold new writing for our stages, cultivating and supporting writers in the UK and around the world, and inspiring the next generation of young theatre-makers.

You can make a one-off donation by text:

Text **Support 5** to 70560 to donate £5

Text **Support 10** to 70560 to donate £10

Text **Support 20** to 70560 to donate £20

Texts cost the donation amount plus one standard message. UK networks only.

To find out more about the different ways in which you can get involved, visit our website: royalcourttheatre.com/support-us

The English Stage Company at the Royal Court Theatre is a registered charity (No. 231242)

WHAT IF IF ONLY

Characters

SOMEONE
FUTURE
FUTURES
PRESENT
CHILD FUTURE

This text went to press before the end of rehearsals and so may differ slightly from the play as performed.

Someone on their own.

SOMEONE

I was reading about this man who spent ten years trying to paint an apple so it looked just like an apple. That was eighteen to twenty eight.

Then he spent seven years trying to paint an apple so it looked nothing like an apple.

Then he died.

This is the sort of thing that interests you. That used to interest you.

I was thinking if he'd lived another ten years what would he have done next. Would he give up painting? Would he kill himself? You know what it takes to kill yourself, would he do that? Maybe he'd start again with an orange.

I was thinking how hard can it be to paint something so it looks nothing like it. You could scribble all over the page. Don't you think?

You could paint the page black.
You could leave the whole page
white. But maybe it had to
somehow be an apple. You could
write apple underneath, maybe not.
I think he was a difficult person like
you're a difficult person. Were. Are.

I was thinking would it always be
the same apple because they'd go
rotten, you never liked the smell of
an apple once it was cut. Did he
paint the apple day by day as it
shrivelled? Or did he always paint
a perfectly ripe apple? Also there's
different kinds of apple. Did he
specialise in a cox or a discovery or
a russet or did he have a go at
different kinds? Braeburn. Bramley.
Winter pearmain.

If I was the one who was dead
would you still be talking to me?
We once said if one of us died if
there was any way of getting in
touch we should do it, I thought
we'd be old. Are you not trying?
If you'd wanted to talk to me you
could have stayed alive.

I've nothing to say really, I just miss
you. I once thought I saw a ghost,
not like King Charles with his
head, just a wisp of something

standing by the door. I've told you
this already, do you remember?
Is remembering something you can
do or has it all gone now? I miss
you I miss you I miss you I miss
you. I miss you. Please, can you?
Just a wisp would be fine. If you
can, please. Please, I miss you.
A small thing, just any small thing,
let me know you're there
somewhere. If you can.

There's someone there.

FUTURE

Yes yes yes yes yes yes yes. Here
I am.

SOMEONE

But you're not you're not have you
turned into there's something I'm
seeing this do you know what it is
what are you?

FUTURE

Of course I'm not, nothing like

SOMEONE

A little like

FUTURE

A little like because you wanted so
much so so so that I felt it I smelt it
I saw it I was it I knew what you
wanted I tasted your what if if only
if only your miss miss missing and
I solidified just enough look you
can't see through me can you, I'm
here I'm almost almost here almost

and you have to help me give you
what you want.

SOMEONE   Can you what bring back can you?

FUTURE   Make your loved one appear make
                 them speak not bring back no
                 make it never have happened that
                 very ghastly not a pretty way to go.
                 I can give you what if if only if
                 only you hadn't something if only
                 they hadn't something all different
                 different I can if you can.

SOMEONE   I will I will tell me what how do I

FUTURE   Make me possible.

SOMEONE   Yes. All right. How? What? See this
                 see this what is it can you see it too
                 are you somewhere are you on the
                 brink of

FUTURE   Because I never happened. Other
                 things happened, things you regret
                 happened, things making you say if
                 only what if

SOMEONE   What are you? You feel like a ghost
                 there's a shiver but you're not
                 you're not I don't want someone
                 else I want

FUTURE   I'm the ghost of a dead future. I'm
                 the ghost of a future that never

happened. And if you can make
me happen then there would be
your beloved real person not a
ghost your real real living because
what happened will never have
happened what happened will be
different will be what you want will
be a happy happy

SOMEONE   But what? how? how do I? just tell
me what

FUTURE   I don't know how, you're the one
living, you're the one who can make
things happen. I'm dead, I'm lucky
to be a ghost, make me happen,
please please. Don't let me go.

SOMEONE   I don't know what to do, tell me,
please

FUTURE   Please please help me make me
happen make me happen

SOMEONE   Please how, make what happen,
how can I, there must be so many
things that didn't happen. I miss
you so much I don't want to mess
this up I don't know what I'm
doing.

FUTURE   Don't don't don't let them all in.
Of course there's so many so many
futures that didn't happen like
drops of rain grains of sand atoms

in your heart. You'll have no peace
if they all come after you and I'm
the best I'm a brilliant Future and
I could easily have happened but
stupid stupid kept choosing the
wrong things and let me die. I'm
a Future you'd really like, everyone
would have liked me if I'd
happened.

SOMEONE   Because you're what?

FUTURE   Equality and cake and no bad bits
at all and I've been glimpsed I've
been died for in China and Russia
and South America and here here
in your little country's history long
ago people wanted me they want
me over and over and forty fifty
years ago I had friends I really
nearly and my enemies say I'm
utopia a nowhere place and I'm
not I needn't be perfect but better
better than what and I never
happen and if I'd happened this
nasty death wouldn't have I'm the
one where it wouldn't I promise
and you've got to make me real
you've got to make me a real live

SOMEONE   Are you the only Future where it
wouldn't or is now the only one
where it did or are there thousands
of ways I can't get my mind round

FUTURE

No no no don't think about the
others the others are hungry to
happen don't let them get a whiff
of your craving stop that stop here
they come

And there's lots of them.

FUTURES

Yes yes yes me me and me and

FUTURE

Don't let them

FUTURES

and me make me the one that
happened me me I'm the favourite
Future silver and white I'm the one
you want you lost the war your
parents were never born you don't
exist silver rockets and robots listen
to me if only don't forget me if
only you hadn't driven and guzzled
and poisoned me me you'd have
tigers and coral don't step on me
look out I'm under your foot
skylarks I'm so small now and slimy
but I could have been could have
been look out I'm the nuclear
nuclear haha give you a fright
I could still no no listen I'm so old
aliens aliens another planet none
of those fires if only listen listen
I can't speak loud I'm so old I can
I can shout because I'm just now
I'm the day you none of that
sickness if only the day you failed

so old so old and they never sailed
and you didn't with me you didn't
fail with me me and they never
wiped out and you never said and
the seas the seas full of fish the
Cherokee president can you hear
me they never killed can you see
me all of me I'm so vast the
asteroid no rule the waves no slaves
if only wiped you all out eek eeek
solved your problem a better better
if only silver and white and me and
faster faster faster till suddenly
what if slow slow and you would
have noticed if only no flies on the
eyes they never they never if only
help me me make me the one that
happened you never if only
butterflies help me your beloved

SOMEONE   Stop stop get off me get out I can't
                   I can't make you be what
                   happened I can't make you happen
                   it's impossible you didn't happen
                   you're nothing nothing you never
                   happened.

                   And they all disappear.

                   Someone else is there.

PRESENT   No, they didn't happen. All gone.
                   Are you all right? You still
                   have one of them in your hair.

Just brush with your fingers, all
gone. I'm the only Future that
didn't die, I'm what's happening
hurrah hello I'm the Present, I'm
here I'm now I'm here I'm now
now now now every second gone
to the past but always here now
now now now. Do you like me?
I'm not very nice not altogether.
So many people sick and dead
and crazy from what I'm like you
know the kind of thing you're
living now now now hello and of
course the wars the Present always
has wars and any Future that
promised no more is dead dead
dead. But there's nice things too
for those who have them, movies
and trees and people who love
each other. Except oops you don't
have that particular one. No, that
one's gone. That one died some
time ago so no longer exists in the
Present, sorry.

SOMEONE   But I thought I hoped

PRESENT   You thought what if if only but all
                  those Futures were dead. None of
                  them happened, you said it
                  yourself, they can't happen.

SOMEONE   But there will be Futures that can
                  happen and maybe

PRESENT   Many many many and just one of
                   them will happen and in none of
                   them will your beloved be there.

SOMEONE   So there's no chance

PRESENT   Not the ghost of a chance. If only.
                   Gone.

SOMEONE   Gone.

PRESENT   Gone.

SOMEONE   Is there a ghost of you, are you
                   somewhere, can you hear this?

PRESENT   Of course not, they're nowhere,
                   gone.

SOMEONE   Do you know this is happening?
                   What do you think?

PRESENT   Nothing nothing they don't think
                   anything. Don't worry, you'll live,
                   you'll go on into the future.
                   Because a Future will come, one of
                   my many many many children,
                   who knows which, maybe better
                   maybe worse, you'll have your little
                   effect on that and it will be the
                   Present as it always is, and the one
                   you miss won't be there. Isn't here.
                   I'm what you've got. Hello, I'm
                   now now now now now can you
                   feel me now?

A small child future is there.

CHILD FUTURE   I'm going to happen.

PRESENT   Here's one of the hopefuls. Do you
want to help it happen?

CHILD FUTURE   I'm going to happen.

SOMEONE   I don't care what happens, not
without

CHILD FUTURE   I want want to happen I'm going to
happen shall I happen?

SOMEONE   Yes no I don't care, yes

PRESENT   Careful, some of them bite, you
don't know what it is.

SOMEONE   What are you then? what will you
be like?

CHILD FUTURE   I'm not telling we never tell, I'm
going to happen.

SOMEONE   And you won't be there. I do know
you've gone.

PRESENT   Gone gone and here I am just
happening now I'm here now hello.

SOMEONE   Gone but I can't stop talking to you
not quite yet. I've seen all these
ghosts do you believe in ghosts
I don't think you did really, you

liked a ghost story that's all. You
liked the same things I liked and
you liked different things and we
liked telling each other about them.
How do I stop talking to you?
Maybe I will sometime but not
now. Is there nothing? Is there a
wisp of you standing by the door?

CHILD FUTURE   I'm going to happen.

End.

AIR

In early 2019, probably around the time I was writing *Imp*, I started each day writing whatever came into my head, not trying to make sense or make it into a play. It did settle into something like dialogue, and after about a dozen I stopped because it began to feel more deliberate and so less interesting.

A year later, as lockdown began, Tom Mothersdale, who I knew as an actor from *Imp*, asked if I had a short piece that could be done in *The Lockdown Plays* he was producing online with Wilf Scolding and Anoushka Warden. I hadn't imagined it being performed, but gave him the first three, which are published here. Three's enough I think. It was performed as a dialogue, and the Berlin Schaubühne website later showed it as a monologue. Take it as you like.

C.C.

Air was first produced as part of *The Lockdown Plays* in May 2020. It was performed by Tom Mothersdale and Lydia Wilson, and directed by Wilf Scolding. *The Lockdown Plays* were created and produced by Tom Mothersdale, Wilf Scolding and Anoushka Warden.

1.

Air. Roses.

But what why where because nothing is happening.

Falling and falling and falling and falling and falling. Into a desert. Give me whatever it is. Did you hear the snow? How it squeaks like a mouse.

Give me the snow.

Not in a little glass globe when you shake it. You can't see through it. Are we on the way to the pole? Are we poles apart? Yesterday I didn't expect this.

I really need

I need to extricate. Backwards. Rewind back to some earlier prehistoric golden childhood imagined okness. Flat feet. Feet like flat fish. They swim on the bottom looking up with their one-sided eyes, up through feet of water, two hundred, double centipede of dark green is it from below?

If I could just hold you still. Motionless and continuing.

I need to be out of this. Out of my skin. Out of my skull. The skeletons dance with no brains in them. A no brainer. What are you touching?

Snow touches, rain touches, air. Roses. Touch inside your nose. I know I'm no rose. I will scream and scream.

How do you completely fill the entire space? Colour the air? It's thick and green. As far as I can see everything's you. As far as I can see.

Holding holding would help. Withholding. You're going back and back. You were a spark in my heart and now whizzing away back up just a star in the sky one of millions my eyes aren't strong enough.

Bread and cake. Whisky and chocolate. Chicken and coffee. Somewhere underground. Far far far. If I bit you?

Out of my skin.

You'll be dead, can I eat you, your eyes, whatever or not. Inside inside your blood, let me, cells and cells mingled. You're alive. Chicken and whisky.

Irremediable. Great gulfs. Fire. Horror movie. Vanish vanish. Scream till everything breaks.

2.

Cacophony caca. Candelabra camomile calamine. Can't.

A weasel is red white and blue. An easel is taken as read.
Easily. This gallery has no slaves. We watched Yugoslavia.
Big slices of meat. And stand forgetting the methane. On
a full stomach full of beans, farting like a bullock.

Butter.

I hear so much about education. Along the river and now
it's low tide. Do you disagree?

So much of it's impossible. Children burnt to death in
their house. Not everyone can be best at the same thing.

Petrol is best. Stormy. Are you someone who thinks the
opposite?

They're all dead to me. We're on the same side, we're on
the side. We're bored. Antimatter is the way to go. When
I feel insecure I want to hit you. How right can I be?

Killing has causes, causes have killing. Causes have causes.
Killing has killing. I hold up my hands and nobody stops.
Pink blue yellow clouds at sunset.

Stricter. Cauterise. Burn the leech off with a cigarette.
Fire the squad. Drown the hanged man. There used to be
medals with coloured ribbons.

Red blue and green and white and blue.

The big ship sailed in the alley alley oh. The plane sailing in the flight path. Eugenics. The nature of the sacrament. How do you pronounce shibboleth? Wait till you see the whites of their eyes. Then decisively eliminate and the world is a solved equation for a blink. I still think I may need to eliminate you.

A toffee apple was a pleasure, two kinds of crunch. From the running.

Running through the grass for elected office. Down. On time. The company. Out.

It slips through my fingers. I love a puzzle, I love a clue, I love a solution, and the dissolution as it dissolves in the solution like salt in the water and I rub my eyes and they smart, I'm not smart enough, and my tears taste salt. If I could shape you, patting the butter, cubing the plasticine, squaring up the pack of cards.

I can believe anything.

I could chop off your fingers. I could chop off my fingers. I can't believe anything.

3.

It seems to be falling horizontally. Did I ever tell you I can taste cubes? Where's the horse?

The mountains look as if they're stuck on. This queasiness.

No one will tell me why. Look, we agreed. What the hell what the fuck.

Green green green. Something for breakfast. Stray cats. Kites too high to see.

Blue and pigeons even so, a paper cut hurts so much too much, is it true he cut off his finger and felt nothing?

We're always shocked.

There's more to it than you think.

I never asked. You will keep going on.

We see them coming round the corner and we duck.

You could climb the scaffolding and easily go from this roof to that roof maybe not.

Do you believe a word they say? Can you hear from here? Can you write with your left hand? Can you phone in gloves? This bar's too full of people I know.

Mind you don't miss the step. I left the umbrella on the bus. So many parakeets and no larks. Red kites have come back. It's closing down. Then you'll be sorry. What was her name?

With a red bandanna? I don't taste colours. Do you imagine any of them naked?

It's a death star. The little man has no legs. It will be all right if you turn it upside down. Give it a shake.

**Other works by Caryl Churchill,
published by Nick Hern Books**

Light Shining in Buckinghamshire
Traps
Cloud Nine
Icecream
Mad Forest
The Skriker
Thyestes (translated from Seneca)
Hotel
This is a Chair
Blue Heart
A Number
A Dream Play (translated from Strindberg)
Drunk Enough to Say I Love You?
Bliss (translated from Olivier Choinière)
Seven Jewish Children
Love and Information
Ding Dong the Wicked
Here We Go
Escaped Alone
Pigs and Dogs
Glass. Kill. Bluebeard's Friends. Imp.

Collections

A Nick Hern Book

What If If Only and *Air* first published in Great Britain as a paperback original in 2021 by Nick Hern Books Limited, The Glasshouse, 49a Goldhawk Road, London W12 8QP, in association with the Royal Court Theatre, London

What If If Only copyright © 2021 Caryl Churchill Limited
Air copyright © 2021 Caryl Churchill Limited

Caryl Churchill has asserted her right to be identified as the author of these works

Designed and typeset by Nick Hern Books
Printed in Great Britain by Mimeo Ltd, Huntingdon, Cambridgeshire PE29 6XX

A CIP catalogue record for this book is available from the British Library

ISBN   978 1 83904 026 9

www.nickhernbooks.co.uk

facebook.com/nickhernbooks

twitter.com/nickhernbooks